Smart Money – A College Student's Guide to Financial Mastery

Author

Danielle A Calise

Table of Contents

Understanding Financial Basics

This chapter will explore the foundational knowledge necessary to develop a strong understanding of personal finance. Financial literacy is crucial for making informed decisions about money, and it is especially important to have a solid grasp of the basics before delving into more complex financial topics.

1.1 The Concept of Money is a medium of exchange that facilitates transactions in our society. It represents the value we assign to goods and services. The history of money dates back to ancient civilizations when bartering was the primary means of trade. As societies evolved, various forms of money emerged. Cash provides immediate purchasing power in the form of physical currency but carries the risk of loss or theft. Credit allows individuals to borrow money to be repaid in the future, providing flexibility, convenience, and the potential for debt. Digital currencies, such as Bitcoin, have gained traction as an alternative form of money in recent years, offering innovative technological solutions built on decentralized systems.

1.2 Establishing Financial Goals Having clear financial objectives is key to creating a solid financial plan. Goals can range from short-term targets, like vacation savings, to long-term goals, such as retirement planning. By defining these goals, individuals can prioritize their spending and saving accordingly. Setting realistic and attainable goals is essential, considering factors such as income, expenses, and time horizons. Moreover, regularly reviewing and adjusting goals is crucial as circumstances change over time.

1.3 Income and Expenses - Understanding income and expenses is crucial for budgeting effectively and creating a sustainable financial situation. Net income refers to the amount of money earned after all taxes and deductions have been taken out. Differentiating between fixed expenses, such as rent, mortgage, or car payments, and variable expenses, such as grocery bills or entertainment, helps individuals allocate their income appropriately. Additionally, discretionary spending refers to non-essential expenses; discretionary income represents the money left over after meeting all necessary costs. Tracking expenses through methods like budgeting apps or spreadsheets can provide valuable insights into spending patterns and help identify areas for potential savings.

1.4 Managing Debt Responsibly - Debt can be helpful when used wisely, such as leveraging a mortgage to acquire a home or taking out a student loan to invest in education. However, it can also become overwhelming if not managed properly. Recognizing the difference between good debt, which may generate future value, and bad debt, characterized by high interest rates on unnecessary purchases, is critical. Strategies like debt consolidation, combining multiple debts into a single loan with a potentially lower interest rate, negotiating lower interest rates, and creating a repayment plan can help individuals minimize and pay off their debt responsibly. Additionally, understanding the impact of credit card debt, which often carries high-interest rates, and making timely payments to avoid late fees and penalties is paramount.

Creating a Budget

Budgeting is an integral part of financial management that enables individuals to take control of their money, achieve financial goals, and make informed decisions about spending and saving. This chapter will delve deeper into creating a budget, exploring various strategies, techniques, and principles to help you develop a comprehensive and practical budget.

1. Assess Your Income:

When assessing your income, consider all sources of money that flow into your life. This includes your primary job salary or wages, income from freelance work or side gigs, rental income, dividends, interest, and any other sources of revenue. Understanding your total income to create an accurate budget is important.

2. Track Your Expenses:

Tracking your expenses helps you gain insight into your spending habits and identifies areas where you may be overspending or making unnecessary purchases. Begin this process by categorizing your expenses into fixed and variable categories. Fixed expenses, such as rent or mortgage payments, utility bills, insurance premiums, and loan repayments, are regular and consistent. Variable expenses, on the other hand, are more flexible and may change from month to month, such as groceries, dining out, entertainment, and personal care products.

To track your expenses effectively, consider utilizing personal finance apps or software that automatically categorize your transactions. Alternatively, maintain a detailed spreadsheet or use a physical expense journal to record your expenditures manually. This step is crucial for understanding where your money is going and helps you evaluate your spending patterns.

3.   Set Financial Goals:

Before diving into the actual budget creation, it is essential to establish clear financial goals. These goals provide direction and purpose to your budget, aligning your spending and saving behaviors accordingly. Financial goals can be short-term (within a year) or long-term (more than a year).

Short-term goals commonly include paying off high-interest debt, saving for a vacation, or purchasing a specific item or gadget. Long-term goals often involve saving for retirement, a down payment on a house, or funding your child's education. Write down your goals and attach a timeframe and a specific monetary value to each. This will give you a benchmark to work towards and enable you to prioritize your spending accordingly.

4. Allocate Your Income:

Allocate your income by dividing it into various budget categories. Start by addressing your fixed expenses, including rent or mortgage payments, utilities, loan payments, insurance premiums, and other regular obligations. These fixed expenses are often the most necessary and less flexible, so deduct them from your income first.

Next, allocate funds towards building an emergency fund and saving for your financial goals. Experts suggest saving 10-20% of your income as a general guideline. Setting aside money for emergencies and future goals ensures you are prepared for unexpected expenses and paves the way toward long-term financial stability.

When allocating funds, using the 50/30/20 budgeting rule can be helpful. This means allocating 50% of your income to needs (fixed expenses), 30% to wants (variable expenses), and 20% to savings and debt repayment. Adjust these percentages based on your own financial goals and circumstances.

Finally, assign a reasonable amount to your discretionary spending categories, such as groceries, dining out, entertainment, clothing, and hobbies. While these categories may offer more flexibility, allocating them mindfully and avoiding excessive spending is still important.

5. Track Your Budget:

Creating a budget is only the beginning; consistently tracking and monitoring your budget is critical to its success. Regularly review your income and expenses to ensure you remain on track with your financial goals and highlight areas that may require adjustments. Evaluate your spending habits and identify any patterns of overspending or potential savings opportunities.

Utilize various tools to track your budget effectively, such as financial management apps, budgeting software, or spreadsheets. These tools visually represent your financial progress and can send alerts or notifications to help you stay within your budgetary limits.

6. Identify Areas for Improvement:

Analyzing your budget and expense tracking may reveal areas where you can improve your financial habits. Look for opportunities to reduce expenses, negotiate bills, and find more affordable alternatives. This might involve meal planning and cooking at home more often, canceling unused subscriptions, or seeking better deals on utilities or insurance.

Boosting your income is another avenue worth exploring. Consider taking on additional freelance work, starting a side business, or investing in passive income streams. Identifying and implementing strategies to increase your earnings can significantly impact your budget's success.

7. Be Flexible:

Keep in mind that life is dynamic and ever-changing. Unexpected expenses, fluctuations in income, or shifts in spending patterns may occur. Staying adaptable and open to adjusting your budget as necessary is vital. In such instances, having an emergency fund becomes crucial, acting as a safety net to cover unexpected costs without derailing your overall financial plan.

8. Seek Professional Help (if needed):

If you struggle with budgeting or need guidance in developing a more advanced financial plan, consider consulting a financial advisor. They can provide expert advice tailored to your specific circumstances and financial goals. A financial advisor can analyze your budget, suggest adjustments, and help you make informed decisions about your money.

Remember, budgeting is an ongoing process that requires dedication and regular assessments. Periodically revisit and update your budget to align with your ever-evolving financial circumstances. By following these steps and maintaining a disciplined approach to budgeting, you can take control of your finances and work towards achieving your short- and long-term goals.

Income Sources

This chapter will explore the various income sources available to individuals. Understanding how to earn money is crucial for financial planning and achieving your goals. Whether you are starting your first job or exploring alternative income streams, this chapter will provide valuable insights and guidance.

1. Employment Income:

    •   Full-time or part-time job: Securing stable employment is often the primary source of income for most individuals. We will discuss the importance of identifying career paths that align with your skills, interests, and financial goals. Moreover, understanding the job market dynamics, such as supply and demand for specific skills, will help make informed decisions about which industries to pursue. Additionally, we will explore strategies for enhancing employability by acquiring relevant certifications, expanding professional networks, and staying updated with industry trends and technology.

2. Self-Employment:

- Entrepreneurship: The entrepreneurial route offers the potential for unlimited income but comes with its own set of challenges. We will delve into starting your own business, including conducting market research to identify viable business opportunities. Developing a comprehensive business plan that outlines the vision, target audience, marketing strategies, financial projections, and scalability will be crucial. Securing funding through sources like bank loans, venture capitalists, or crowdfunding platforms will also be discussed. Furthermore, understanding legal obligations, such as registering your business, obtaining licenses and permits, and complying with tax regulations, is essential to operate successfully.

3. Investments and Dividends:

- Stocks, Bonds, and Mutual Funds:
  Investing in financial markets can
  provide a passive income stream. We
  will delve deeper into stocks, bonds,
  and mutual funds, explaining their
  differences, benefits, and risks.
  Understanding fundamental and
  technical analysis will aid in making
  informed investment decisions.
  Furthermore, exploring investment
  strategies such as value, growth, and
  index investing will help individuals
  tailor their portfolios to risk tolerance
  and investment goals. Additionally, we
  will discuss the significance of
  diversification, asset allocation, and
  rebalancing to ensure a well-rounded
  investment portfolio.

4. Rental Income and Real Estate:

- Property Investments: Real estate can
  be an excellent source of income
  through rental properties or real estate

investments. We will explore the process of investing in rental properties, including conducting due diligence on the property, analyzing the rental market, and assessing potential rental income. Strategies for financing your real estate investments, such as obtaining mortgages or partnering with investors, will be discussed. Understanding property management techniques, tenant screening, lease agreements, and maintenance and repairs will also be covered. Moreover, we will discuss the potential benefits of real estate investment trusts (REITs) and real estate crowdfunding as alternatives to direct property ownership.

5. Passive Income:

- Royalties and Licensing: Generating passive income through royalties and licensing can be achieved through various creative pursuits. For writers, this could involve publishing books, e-books, or audiobooks. We will explore the publishing process in more depth, including self-publishing options, traditional publishing routes, and the emerging field of digital publishing. Tips for crafting compelling content, building an author platform, and navigating the ever-evolving landscape of book marketing will be emphasized. Additionally, we will discuss the importance of copyright protection, negotiating contracts, and leveraging digital platforms for broader reach. Furthermore, we will touch upon the potential of passive income through licensing intellectual property, such as music, artwork, or inventions, and the steps involved in securing licensing deals.

6. Side Hustles:

- Additional Income Streams: Side hustles are popular for supplementing your primary income. We will provide an expanded list of side hustle ideas, including online tutoring, affiliate marketing, dropshipping, content creation, event planning, freelance photography, web design, and many more. Exploring various platforms, marketplaces, and gig economy apps that connect individuals with these side hustle opportunities will be highlighted. Furthermore, we will discuss the importance of time management, marketing strategies, and expanding skills to create a sustainable and scalable side hustle. Tips and strategies for transitioning side hustles into full-time ventures for those seeking entrepreneurship will also be provided.

7. Gig Economy:

*   Freelancing and Temporary Work: The gig economy has recently grown, offering individuals flexible and independent work opportunities. We will provide a comprehensive overview of popular gig economy platforms, including Upwork, Fiverr, TaskRabbit,

and Uber, and how to effectively leverage them to secure freelancing or contract work. Moreover, we will discuss the importance of building a solid personal brand, creating a compelling portfolio, and networking within gig economy communities to enhance visibility and attract clients. Strategies for managing multiple gigs, setting realistic rates, and ensuring a steady income stream will also be addressed. Additionally, we will explore emerging sectors within the gig economy, such as virtual assistance, social media management, and online coaching.

8. Passive Investments:

- Index Funds, Mutual Funds, and Real Estate Crowdfunding: Passive investments offer a hands-off approach to investing while providing exposure to a diversified portfolio. We will delve deeper into the benefits and risks of index funds and mutual funds, explaining concepts such as expense ratios, asset allocation, and rebalancing. Exploring various investment platforms, such as brokerage accounts, robo-advisors, and retirement accounts, will aid in selecting the best options for individual needs. Additionally, we will discuss the emerging trend of real estate crowdfunding, which allows individuals to invest in real estate projects with smaller capital commitments. Understanding the due diligence process, analyzing potential returns, and assessing the credibility of crowdfunding platforms will be covered. Moreover, we will explore the pros and cons of real estate crowdfunding compared to direct property ownership or REITs.

This chapter delved into these income sources in greater depth, providing valuable information, tips, and strategies to help you navigate and make the most of your financial opportunities. Remember, building multiple income streams can help provide financial security and flexibility in the long run.

Managing Expenses

This chapter will dive deeper into the vital aspect of managing expenses effectively. As a writer, it is crucial to be mindful of your finances and ensure that your expenses align with your income. By implementing intelligent strategies and making thoughtful choices, you can maintain financial stability and focus on your writing career.

1.   Assessing Your Current Expenses:

To understand your financial situation comprehensively, it is essential to assess your current expenses thoroughly. This entails evaluating essential costs, including rent, utilities, groceries, transportation, healthcare, and discretionary spending, such as entertainment, dining out, travel, and hobbies.

Begin by tracking these expenses for at least a month to understand clearly where your money is going. Utilize budgeting apps or spreadsheets to categorize your expenses and analyze patterns. This process will offer a realistic picture of your spending habits and allow you to identify areas where you can adjust. I suggest remembering payments you make quarterly, biannually, and annually so that you may set aside money monthly for this "balloon" type of expense. Examples of these would include insurance premiums, software licenses, etc.

When assessing your expenses, consider your financial goals and priorities. Are you saving for a down payment on a house, investing in your writing education, or planning for retirement? Understanding your larger objectives will give you a better perspective on where to focus your resources and make necessary adjustments.

2. Creating a Realistic Budget:

Based on your assessment, creating a realistic budget that accurately reflects your income and expenses is crucial. A budget is a financial blueprint that empowers you to allocate your resources effectively. It helps you establish boundaries for your spending, ensure that your expenses are sustainable, and provide a roadmap for achieving your financial goals.

As you create your budget, set limits for each spending category and allocate enough funds for essential expenses while keeping discretionary spending in check. Aim for a balance that allows you to enjoy your life while also saving for future goals. Finding a middle ground between being frugal and enjoying the present moment is important.

Prioritize your expenses, ensuring that you cover necessities like rent, utilities, groceries, transportation, and healthcare first. Then, allocate funds for savings, writing-related expenses (e.g., courses, conferences, self-publishing costs), debt repayments, and discretionary spending. Remember that priorities vary from person to person, so tailor your budget to align with your specific circumstances and financial objectives.

3. Cutting Back on Non-Essential Expenses:

To maximize your financial resources, you must be mindful of your discretionary spending and identify areas where you can make cuts without sacrificing too much. This step involves taking a closer look at your habits and being willing to make thoughtful choices.

Evaluate your discretionary spending and seek opportunities to reduce expenses. For example, consider reducing the frequency of dining out or opting for more cost-effective alternatives for entertainment. Reviewing your subscriptions (e.g., streaming services, magazines), gym memberships, and other recurring expenses might also be helpful to ensure they align with your priorities.

One effective strategy is implementing the "30-day rule" for non-essential purchases. Whenever you feel the urge to buy something, wait for 30 days. During this period, evaluate whether the purchase is necessary or if the desire fades over time. This rule helps you distinguish between impulsive spending and intentional purchases aligned with your values.

4. Exploring Cost-Saving Strategies:

To optimize your expenses, consider various cost-saving strategies that can help you stretch your dollars further. Look for discounts, coupons, or loyalty programs to save money on essentials like groceries, clothing, or household items. A little effort in seeking out these opportunities can result in significant savings over time.

Additionally, explore ways to reduce recurring expenses. Negotiate lower rates for utilities or insurance by shopping around and comparing options. Consolidating debt or refinancing loans might help lower monthly payments or interest rates, relieving your monthly financial obligations.

Collaborating with others can also help alleviate financial burdens. Consider sharing expenses with roommates or fellow writers in a writing group for rent, utilities, or retreats. This reduces costs and fosters a supportive community where you can share ideas and collaborate creatively.

Take advantage of technology to further save on writing-related costs. Use free writing software like Google Docs or open-source programs like LibreOffice. Leverage online resources for research instead of buying expensive books or subscribing to paid databases. When purchasing necessary equipment or software, explore affordable options or consider buying gently used items.

5. Reviewing and Adjusting Your Budget:

Creating a budget is not a one-time task; it requires regular review and adjustment to ensure it remains effective and aligned with your changing circumstances. Set aside time each month or quarter to review your budget and track your expenses diligently.

During these reviews, analyze your spending patterns and compare them against your budgeted amounts. Identify any areas where you are consistently overspending or areas where you can further cut back. Making adjustments promptly will help you stay on track and prevent any financial surprises.

Life circumstances may change, and it's crucial to be prepared to modify your budget accordingly. For example, if you experience a decreased income or face unexpected expenses, reevaluate your budget to accommodate these changes. Flexibility is key to ensuring your budget remains realistic and adaptable.

Take advantage of insights gained during budget reviews. For example, if you consistently overspend on dining out, consider meal prepping or exploring new recipes to reduce costs while enjoying delicious meals. Involve family members or roommates in discussions about budget priorities, fostering a sense of shared responsibility and accountability.

6. Building an Emergency Fund:

Establishing an emergency fund is even more important to mitigate financial uncertainties. An emergency fund acts as a financial safety net, providing stability during challenging times and allowing you to focus on your writing without excessive worry about immediate financial pressures.

Aim to save at least three to six months' living expenses in your emergency fund. Start small by setting aside a certain percentage of your income each month. Consider setting up an automatic transfer to a separate account designated for emergencies. This automates the saving process, ensuring consistency and discipline in building your emergency fund.

Think of your emergency fund as an investment in your financial well-being. It offers peace of mind, protecting you from unexpected expenses, income fluctuations, or emergencies. Beyond its immediate security, having an emergency fund allows you to pursue your writing goals without constantly living on the edge of financial stress.

7. Seeking Opportunities for Additional Income:

While managing expenses is crucial, increasing your income can also significantly impact your financial stability. Explore ways to supplement your income with additional sources of revenue. This can involve taking on freelance writing gigs or part-time jobs or leveraging your skills to offer tutoring, editing, proofreading, or ghostwriting services.

However, it is essential to strike a balance that allows you to maintain your focus on school. While additional income streams can provide stability, ensure they do not compromise the quality or quantity of your study time.

Effectively managing your expenses is paramount to your financial stability. By thoroughly assessing your current costs and creating a realistic budget, you can gain control over your finances and ensure that your expenses align with your income. Reducing non-essential expenses and exploring cost-saving strategies will help you stretch your dollars further and maximize your resources.

Regularly reviewing and adjusting your budget is essential to stay on track and adapt to any changes in your financial situation. Life circumstances may change, and it is crucial to be flexible and adjust your budget as needed. This will help you maintain financial stability and ensure your budget remains realistic and adaptable.

One key aspect of managing expenses is building an emergency fund. An emergency fund mitigates financial uncertainties as a student's income fluctuates. Aim to save at least three to six months' living expenses in your emergency fund. This will provide a financial safety net and allow you to focus on your writing without excessive worry about immediate financial pressures.

In addition to managing expenses, seeking opportunities for additional income can significantly impact your financial stability. Look for ways to supplement your writing income, such as freelancing or offering writing-related services. Networking and marketing yourself can lead to potential writing assignments or collaborations, expanding your creative and financial opportunities.

Managing expenses effectively is crucial for your financial well-being as a writer. By assessing your current expenses, creating a realistic budget, cutting back on non-essential expenses, exploring cost-saving strategies, reviewing and adjusting your budget regularly, building an emergency fund, and seeking opportunities for additional income, you can maintain financial stability and focus on your writing career with peace of mind.

Financial Aid and Loans

This chapter will delve into financial aid and loans, exploring the intricacies of these crucial resources that help students afford college education. College tuition costs can be overwhelming, but luckily, several options are available to assist students in financing their education.

Let's start by exploring the different types of financial aid available. Scholarships, grants, and work-study programs are among the most common forms of financial assistance.

Scholarships are awarded based on merit, considering factors such as academic achievements, talents, or special skills. They can be provided by the college or university itself, private organizations, or individual donors. Scholarships can cover a portion or the entirety of tuition fees, and numerous scholarship databases and search engines are available online to help students find and apply for these opportunities.

Grants, on the other hand, are often need-based and are awarded based on a student's financial circumstances. These grants can come from federal or state governments, colleges, or specific organizations. Filling out the Free Application for Federal Student Aid (FAFSA) is crucial as it is essential in determining your eligibility for federal grants, such as the Pell Grant. Additionally, colleges and universities may have institutional grants based on financial need or specific criteria.

Work-study programs allow students to work part-time on campus, helping them cover their expenses while gaining valuable work experience. These programs are typically funded by federal or state governments and are offered to students who demonstrate financial need. Work-study positions can range from working in the library or administrative offices to assisting faculty members with research projects. The funds earned from these positions are often used towards educational expenses or living costs. It's important to note that work-study earnings do not count against you in future financial aid applications, as they are considered need-based aid rather than income.

When it comes to student loans, understanding the various options and their implications is vital. The primary types of student loans include federal, private, and parent loans.

Federal loans are generally more favorable due to their lower interest rates and flexible repayment options. They can be subsidized, meaning the government covers the interest while the borrower is in school, or unsubsidized, where interest accrues when the loan is disbursed. The most common types of federal loans are Stafford Loans and Perkins Loans. Stafford Loans are available to undergraduate and graduate students, and they come in both subsidized and unsubsidized forms. Perkins Loans are need-based and have a fixed interest rate. Both federal loans have annual and lifetime borrowing limits, varying depending on your grade level and dependency status.

On the other hand, private lenders, such as banks or credit unions, offer personal loans. While private loans can provide additional funds for education, they tend to have higher interest rates and more stringent repayment terms than federal loans. Borrowers may need a co-signer with good credit to secure a private loan, and repayment usually begins while the borrower is still in school.

Parents can also take out loans to help finance their child's education. The Parent PLUS Loan is a federal loan that allows parents of dependent undergraduate students to borrow money to cover any remaining costs after applying for financial aid. These loans have a higher interest rate than other federal loans but offer flexible repayment plans.

It is crucial to thoroughly research and compare different loan options before committing to one. Understanding interest rates, repayment plans, and deferment options will help you make informed decisions. Some federal loans offer income-driven repayment plans, which adjust your monthly payments based on your income and family size. Public service loan forgiveness programs are also available for borrowers who work in specific eligible fields, such as government or non-profit organizations. Exploring these options early on can significantly impact your post-graduation financial stability.

When applying for student loans, attention to detail is essential. Filling out the FAFSA accurately and on time is crucial as it determines your eligibility for federal aid. Pay attention to loan terms and conditions, including repayment start dates, interest rates, and origination fees. Calculating the total cost of borrowing and weighing it against your expected future earnings are crucial to ensure manageable loan payments after graduation.

Loan forgiveness programs provide relief for borrowers burdened with significant loan debt. These programs generally require a commitment to working in specific fields, such as education, healthcare, or public service, for a certain period. For example, the Public Service Loan Forgiveness program forgives remaining loan balances after 120 qualifying payments for full-time individuals for qualifying employers. Some states also offer loan forgiveness programs for certain professions or in exchange for community service.

Managing loan repayment effectively is key to maintaining financial stability. Create a repayment plan that aligns with your financial situation and goals, taking into account your income, expenses, and other financial commitments. Explore loan consolidation or refinancing options to simplify payments and potentially lower interest rates. Additionally, be aware of the consequences of defaulting on your loans, as it can damage your credit score and lead to wage garnishment or other forms of legal action.

Navigating financial aid and loans is essential to the college experience. Students can make informed decisions about financing their education while minimizing long-term financial burdens by understanding the different types of financial aid available, the intricacies of student loans, and the potential benefits of loan forgiveness programs. It's crucial to approach financial assistance and loans with careful consideration, proactive planning, and a focus on long-term financial well-being.

Credit and Debt Management

In today's society, credit plays a significant role in our financial lives. From purchasing a car to buying a home, having good credit is essential. However, if not managed properly, credit can quickly become a burden and lead to mounting debt. This chapter will explore the importance of credit and how to manage it responsibly to avoid financial distress.

Section 1: Understanding Credit Scores

1.1 Definition and Purpose of Credit Scores Credit scores are numerical representations of an individual's creditworthiness. Lenders use these scores to assess the likelihood of repayment when considering issuing credit or loans.

1.2 Factors Influencing Credit Scores To understand credit scores better, it's vital to be aware of the factors that impact them: - Payment history: This factor carries significant weight. Consistently making on-time payments positively affects your credit score. - Utilization ratio refers to the amount of credit you currently use compared to your total credit limit. Keeping this ratio low, ideally below 30%, positively affects your credit score. - Length of credit history: Lenders prefer borrowers with a more extended credit history, as it provides a more comprehensive picture of their reliability. - Types of credit: A mix of credit accounts, such as credit cards, auto loans, and mortgages, can positively influence your credit score. - Credit inquiries: Applying for multiple credit accounts within a short period can negatively impact your credit score.

Section 2: Building and Establishing Credit

2.1 Building Credit for Individuals with No Credit History Getting started with credit can be challenging when you have no credit history. Here are some strategies to establish credit: - Apply for a secured credit card. Secured credit cards require a cash deposit as collateral, making them accessible for those just starting to build credit. - Become an authorized user: By becoming an authorized user on someone else's credit card, their positive payment history can be reflected on your credit report. - Obtain a credit builder loan: Some financial institutions offer specialized loans to help individuals establish credit.

2.2 Tips for Managing Credit Responsibly Once you have access to credit, it's crucial to manage it responsibly. Here are some best practices: - Make all payments on time: Late payments can significantly negatively impact your credit score. Set up automatic payments or reminders to help you make timely payments. - Keep credit utilization low: Aim to use less than 30% of your total available credit. High credit utilization may indicate financial strain to lenders. - Avoid opening multiple accounts within a short period: Rapidly opening new credit accounts can make you appear risky to lenders and may negatively affect your credit score.

Section 3: Managing Credit Card Debt

3.1 Understanding the Dangers of High-Interest Credit Card Debt High-interest credit card debt can quickly accumulate and become challenging due to interest charges. Minimum payments may only cover interest, keeping borrowers in a perpetual cycle of debt.

3.2 Creating a Debt Repayment Plan To tackle credit card debt effectively, follow these steps: - List all credit card debts, interest rates, and minimum payments. - Prioritize debts: Consider the debt with the highest interest rate or the smallest balance. - Explore repayment methods: Two popular strategies include the avalanche method (paying off high-interest debt first) and the snowball method (paying off low-balance debts first).

3.3 Strategies for Reducing Credit Card Debt When reducing credit card debt, consider the following strategies: - Increase monthly payments: Allocate more money towards paying off the debt each month. Even small additional payments can have a significant impact on reducing the balance over time. - Negotiate lower interest rates: Contact credit card companies to request reduced interest rates. Explain your situation and demonstrate responsible payment behavior. - Consider balance transfers: Transfer high-interest credit card balances to a new card with a lower interest rate. Be cautious of transfer fees and ensure that the lower rate is applicable for a significant period. - Seek professional help: If managing credit card debt becomes overwhelming, credit counseling agencies can assist in negotiating lower interest rates and developing a repayment plan.

Section 4: Dealing with Student Loans

4.1 Understanding the Various Types of Student Loans Student loans come in two primary types: - Federal student loans, Offered through the government with fixed interest rates and flexible repayment options. - Private student loans: Obtained through banks, credit unions, or online lenders, often with higher interest rates and limited repayment options.

4.2 Exploring Repayment Options and Loan Forgiveness Programs There are several repayment options and loan forgiveness programs available for student loan borrowers: - Income-driven repayment plans: These plans adjust monthly payments based on income and family size. - Public Service Loan Forgiveness (PSLF): Individuals working full-time for a qualifying employer may be eligible for loan forgiveness after making 120 qualifying payments. - Teacher Loan

Forgiveness: Teachers in high-need areas may qualify for loan forgiveness after meeting specific criteria.

4.3 Strategies for Managing Student Loan Payments To manage student loan payments effectively, consider these strategies: - Create a budget: Determine how much you can allocate towards monthly loan payments. - Consider refinancing: Explore options for refinancing your student loans at a lower interest rate to reduce monthly payments potentially. - Communicate with loan servicers: If facing financial hardships, discuss deferment, forbearance, or alternative repayment plans that offer temporary relief.

Section 5: Debt Consolidation and Negotiation

5.1 Exploring the Option of Debt Consolidation combines multiple debts into a single loan with a lower interest rate. It simplifies payments and may potentially lower monthly expenses. However, comparing consolidation options and assessing the associated costs is crucial.

5.2 Understanding Debt Negotiation or Settlement Debt negotiation or settlement involves negotiating with creditors to reduce the overall amount owed. It's essential to be cautious as debt settlement can have long-term consequences, such as a negative impact on credit scores.

Section 6: Credit Counseling and Repair

6.1 When to Seek Professional Credit Counseling Services Consider seeking professional credit counseling services if you experience: - Difficulty managing debt independently. - There is a need for assistance in creating a budget and repayment plan. - Facing creditor lawsuits or threats of foreclosure.

6.2 Tips for Choosing a Reputable Credit Counseling Agency When choosing a credit counseling agency, consider the following tips: - Research and select a nonprofit agency affiliated with reputable industry organizations. - Verify their credentials, certifications, and reputation through consumer protection agencies. - Understand the fees involved and ensure they are reasonable and transparent.

6.3 Understanding Credit Repair Services Credit repair companies claim to fix negative items on credit reports but cannot remove accurate information. Be cautious of scams and companies that promise unrealistic results. Reviewing your credit reports regularly and disputing any errors promptly can help improve your credit standing.

Section 7: Avoiding Bad Credit Habits

7.1 Common Mistakes to Avoid To maintain good credit habits, avoid the following mistakes: - Overspending: Avoid splurging beyond your means and relying too heavily on credit to finance your purchases. - Missing payments: Always make your payments on time to avoid late fees and negative impacts on your credit score. - Maxing out credit cards: Keeping your credit utilization ratio low is crucial for maintaining a good credit score. - Applying for too much credit: Each time you apply for credit, it can result in a hard inquiry on your credit report, temporarily lowering your credit score. - Ignoring your credit report: Regularly check it for errors and discrepancies and take steps to correct them.

7.2 Establishing and Maintaining Good Credit Habits To establish and maintain good credit habits, follow these practices: - Pay your bills on time: Make all payments, including credit card bills, loan payments, and utility bills, on or before the due date. - Keep your credit utilization low: Aim to use no more than 30% of your available credit to keep your credit utilization ratio in check. - Monitor your credit regularly: Check your credit report at least once a year to ensure accuracy and identify potential issues. - Diversify your credit mix: A mix of credit accounts, such as credit cards, loans, and mortgages, can positively impact your credit score. - Limit new credit applications: Applying for credit too frequently can raise red flags for lenders, so be mindful of how often you seek new credit.

Section 8: Protecting Yourself from Identity Theft

8.1 Understanding Identity Theft Identity theft occurs when someone steals your personal information to commit fraud.

8.2 Protecting Your Personal and Financial Information To protect yourself from identity theft, follow these steps: - Safeguard personal documents: Store important documents, such as passports, social security cards, and bank statements, in a safe place. - Shred sensitive documents contain personal and financial information before they are disposed of. - Use strong passwords: Create strong passwords for your online accounts and avoid using the same password for multiple accounts. - Be cautious online: Avoid clicking on suspicious links or providing personal information to unknown websites or individuals. - Monitor your accounts: Regularly review your bank and credit card statements for unauthorized transactions.

8.3 What to Do if You Become a Victim of Identity Theft If you suspect you have been a victim of identity theft, take the following steps: - Contact the authorities: Report the identity theft to the police and file an identity theft report. - Notify financial institutions: Contact your bank, credit card companies, and any other relevant financial institutions to report the fraudulent activity. - Place a fraud alert or freeze on your credit report: This will help prevent further unauthorized accounts or activities. - Monitor your accounts: Keep a close eye on your accounts for any additional signs of fraudulent activity. - Keep detailed records: Document all interactions and actions taken to resolve the identity theft.

Understanding and managing credit and debt are essential aspects of financial responsibility. You can ensure a healthy financial future by maintaining good credit habits, effectively managing credit card debt, and staying vigilant against identity theft. Responsible credit and debt management can open doors for future opportunities and financial stability.

Saving and Investing: Building a Strong Financial Foundation

In an increasingly uncertain and rapidly changing world, the importance of saving and investing for our financial future cannot be stressed enough. As a famous writer, I encourage my readers to delve deeper into this topic, exploring the intricacies and nuances of saving and investing. We can secure a comfortable and prosperous future by adopting a holistic and long-term perspective and making insightful financial decisions.

Understanding the Benefits of Saving Money

Saving money provides us with a sense of financial security and stability. It acts as a safety net, allowing us to navigate through unexpected expenses and financial hardships without resorting to debt. However, the benefits of saving extend far beyond mere emergency funds. Saving enables us to fulfill future goals and aspirations, such as purchasing a home, funding education, taking a dream vacation, or even starting a business. It empowers us to create our desired life and brings us closer to financial independence.

Setting Realistic Saving Goals

To effectively save, it is crucial to set realistic and attainable goals. Begin by identifying what you are saving for short-term expenses, long-term investments, or retirement. Break down your goals into smaller milestones, giving yourself a clear roadmap towards success. By setting achievable targets, you'll find it easier to track your progress and stay motivated. Consider creating a vision board or using digital tools that visualize your goals, reminding you of what you're working towards and why it matters.

Budgeting: The Foundation of Successful Saving

Creating a budget is an essential step in the saving process. Start by assessing your income and expenses and allocating funds for essential needs such as housing, utilities, transportation, and healthcare. Be mindful of discretionary expenses and differentiate between wants and needs. Realize that every dollar spent frivolously is a missed opportunity for saving and investing in your future. Track your spending habits meticulously, identifying areas where you can cut costs and be more mindful of your financial choices. By examining your budget closely, you can redirect funds towards savings without sacrificing your quality of life.

Automating Savings: A Foolproof Strategy

Automating savings is a powerful technique for cultivating consistent saving habits. By establishing automatic transfers from your checking account to a savings account or investment account, you can effortlessly allocate a portion of your income toward your financial goals each month. This proactive approach to saving removes the temptation to spend excess funds, reinforcing discipline and responsibility. You'll be pleasantly surprised by the impact of small, consistent contributions as they accumulate over time.

The Magnificent Power of Compound Interest

One of the most intriguing aspects of saving is compound interest. You can benefit from the magic of compounding over time by depositing money in interest-earning savings accounts or investments. Compound interest allows your initial savings to grow exponentially as the interest earned is added to the principal amount. To maximize the impact of compound interest, start your savings journey as early as possible. The longer your money compounds, the more substantial your returns will be. Embrace this financial superpower and witness the true potential of your savings.

Investing: Growing Your Wealth for a Brighter Future

While saving focuses on preserving funds, investing is about putting your money to work to generate returns and grow wealth. Investing is vital to financial success, allowing you to achieve long-term financial goals beyond what saving alone can accomplish. However, investing does involve varying degrees of risk, and understanding your risk tolerance is crucial before delving into the world of investments.

Unveiling Different Investment Options

Numerous investment options are available, each with unique characteristics and risk profiles. Stocks represent ownership in a company, providing potential capital appreciation and dividend income. On the other hand, bonds are debt securities issued by governments or corporations, offering fixed interest payments over a specified period. Mutual funds pool money from multiple investors to invest in diversified portfolios of stocks, bonds, or other assets. Real estate offers the potential for appreciation, rental income, and tax advantages. Each investment option should be carefully considered based on financial goals, risk tolerance, and available resources.

Diversification: Minimizing Risk in Investing

Diversification is a cornerstone principle of investing that helps minimize risk. By spreading your investments across different asset classes, sectors, and geographic regions, you reduce the impact of market fluctuations. Different investments tend to perform differently under various conditions. Thus, diversifying your portfolio mitigates the potential for significant loss if one investment underperforms. By striking a balance between various investments, you create a risk-optimized portfolio that increases the likelihood of long-term success.

Evaluating Risk Tolerance and Managing Emotions

Before embarking on any investment journey, it is paramount to assess your risk tolerance. Factors such as your age, financial goals, time horizon, and personal circumstances influence your ability and willingness to withstand fluctuations in the value of your investments. Conduct a thorough risk tolerance assessment to align your investments with your comfort level, ensuring you stay calm and steadfast even during market downturns. Additionally, managing your emotions is crucial. Investor psychology often leads to irrational behavior when markets fluctuate. Staying disciplined, avoiding emotional reactions to market volatility, and relying on well-informed strategies are key to long-term investment success.

Research: An Essential Tool for Informed Investing

Thorough research is paramount to making informed investment decisions. Dive into the financial health, competitive position, and historical performance of the companies or assets you are considering. Analyze annual reports, financial statements, and analyst reports to gather valuable insights. Keep a close eye on market trends, economic indicators, and geopolitical events that can impact your investments. This commitment to research will enable you to make well-informed decisions and build a robust investment portfolio.

Learning From Investment Mistakes

No investment journey is without its share of mistakes and setbacks. What truly matters is how we adapt and learn from these experiences. Accept that losses might occur, and use them to reflect on your strategy, learn from your missteps, and refine your investment approach. The knowledge gained from investing, whether positive or negative, empowers you to make better financial decisions in the future. Embrace these lessons and grow both financially and personally.

Secure Your Future: Retirement Planning

Retirement planning deserves special attention when it comes to saving and investing. It is crucial to save for retirement early on to ensure financial security in your later years. Take advantage of retirement savings accounts such as 401(k)s or Individual Retirement Accounts (IRAs) that offer tax advantages and potential employer matching contributions. Contribute consistently to these accounts, increasing your savings over time. Diversify investments within your retirement portfolio, aligning them with your risk tolerance and long-term retirement goals.

Saving and investing pave the way to financial success and security. By following the guidance in this chapter and continuously building upon your knowledge, you are shaping a solid financial foundation. Remember, saving and investing are not short-term solutions but lifelong commitments. Cultivate patience, discipline, and a willingness to make informed decisions. Your choices today will undoubtedly shape your financial future. Start saving and investing wisely to secure your financial success and achieve the life you envision.

Life After College

Once you graduate from college, a new and exciting chapter of your life begins. Life after college can be exhilarating and overwhelming as you transition from student life to the professional world. In this extended chapter, we will delve deeper into important aspects to consider and provide valuable advice to help you thrive in this transformative phase.

1. Crafting an Effective Job Search Strategy: Finding your first job after college can be challenging, but with a well-thought-out strategy, you can increase your chances of success. Start by identifying your unique skills, strengths, and interests. Understand the industries or specific roles that align with your aspirations and research in-demand job markets. To explore potential opportunities, utilize multiple resources such as networking events, online job portals, and career fairs. Leverage your college's career services department, alum network, and social media platforms like LinkedIn to

60

connect with professionals in your field. Additionally, consider interning or volunteering to gain practical experience and expand your network while adding value to your resume.

2. Mastering the Art of Interview Preparation: Once you secure job interviews, it is crucial to be well-prepared to make a favorable impression. Start by thoroughly researching the company's mission, values, and recent projects. Understand its culture to assess if it aligns with your values and goals. This knowledge will enable you to tailor your answers and showcase your enthusiasm for the organization during the interview. Practice common interview questions, anticipate behavioral or situational questions, and prepare compelling examples demonstrating your problem-solving abilities and achievements. Consider conducting mock interviews with a friend or mentor to refine your responses and gain confidence. Rehearse your elevator pitch,

highlighting your unique skills and experiences that set you apart. Moreover, don't forget to ask thoughtful questions about the position and the company to leave a lasting impression.

3. Navigating the Workplace Dynamics: Starting a new job can be intimidating, but you can integrate smoothly by understanding and adapting to the workplace environment. Observe and learn from your coworkers and supervisors, paying attention to the office culture, communication styles, and expectations. Be proactive in building relationships by initiating conversations and offering assistance to colleagues. Seek opportunities to collaborate and contribute, showcasing your active participation as a team player. As a newcomer, demonstrating your willingness to learn and adapt will make a positive impression. Moreover, adopt a proactive approach to your professional development by seeking growth opportunities, attending training

programs, and staying up-to-date with advancements in your industry.

4. Managing Finances Wisely: As you transition to a full-time job, developing and maintaining strong financial habits from the outset is vital. Start by creating a comprehensive post-college budget considering essential expenses such as rent, utilities, groceries, transportation, and student loan payments. Prioritize building an emergency fund to handle unforeseen expenses and contribute to retirement savings early. Understand your employee benefits, such as health insurance plans, retirement plans, and flexible spending accounts, to make informed decisions and maximize their value. Be cautious of unnecessary debt and exercise responsible credit card usage. Seek guidance from financial advisors or attend workshops that provide insights on budgeting, investing, and managing your financial future effectively.

5. Embracing Lifelong Learning and Professional Development: Learning does not end after college; it is an ongoing process crucial for career advancement. Stay updated on industry trends and new developments by subscribing to trade publications, attending webinars, podcasts, and conferences, and joining professional associations. Consider obtaining industry certifications or licenses that enhance marketability and open doors to growth opportunities. Seek mentors who can provide guidance, support, and valuable insights specific to your field. Actively engage in online and offline professional networks, leveraging platforms like LinkedIn to connect with professionals across various industries. Continuously seek ways to expand your knowledge, skills, and expertise to remain competitive in a changing job market.

6. Prioritizing Work-Life Balance: A healthy work-life balance is essential for your overall well-being and success

in your career. While it may be tempting to immerse yourself fully in your work, it is crucial to establish boundaries to prevent burnout. Allocate dedicated time for hobbies, exercise, social activities, and relaxation. Practice effective time management and prioritize tasks to maintain productivity and reduce stress. Disconnect from work during your personal time, allowing yourself to recharge and enjoy meaningful relationships. Remember that a balanced lifestyle enhances your personal life and improves workplace performance, creativity, and satisfaction.

7. Cultivating Professional Relationships and Effective Networking: Networking is an invaluable asset in any career. Nurture and expand your professional relationships both online and offline. Attend industry-related events and conferences to connect with like-minded individuals, potential mentors, and employers. Join professional associations and engage in their

activities and committees to build a strong network within your industry. Actively participate in conversations, share your insights, and offer support to others. Seek mentorship opportunities from seasoned professionals who can guide and share their experiences. These relationships can open doors to meaningful career opportunities, collaborations, and growth.

8.   Embracing Change, Adaptability, and Personal Growth: Life after college is a time of profound growth and change. Embrace these opportunities by seeking new challenges that push you beyond your comfort zone. Pursue professional development opportunities, take on cross-functional responsibilities, or explore side projects that allow you to expand your skill set. Be open to feedback and constructive criticism, as they provide valuable insights for continuous improvement. Cultivate a growth mindset, always seeking new knowledge, skills, and perspectives.

Through adaptability, resilience, and a willingness to embrace change, you can navigate the uncertainties of the post-college world and chart an exciting and fulfilling career path.

As you embark on life after college, remember this journey is unique. Embrace the challenges and opportunities that come your way, and approach them confidently and willing to learn and grow. Believe in your abilities, stay adaptable, and never stop pursuing your passions and aspirations. This chapter marks the beginning of an incredible adventure where you have the power to shape your success and make a meaningful impact in your chosen field.

Emergency Planning

Emergencies can occur unexpectedly and can have a significant impact on your financial stability. It is crucial to have a well-thought-out emergency plan in place to help mitigate the financial consequences of unforeseen events. This chapter will explore different aspects of emergency planning and how to prepare yourself for potential emergencies.

1. Building an Emergency Fund:

1.1 The importance of having an emergency fund - An emergency fund acts as a financial safety net, providing you with the necessary funds to cover unexpected expenses without disrupting your regular budget. It can help you avoid going into debt or dipping into investments during tough times. - Unexpected expenses include medical emergencies, car repairs, home repairs, job loss, or even natural disasters. Having funds readily available can help you navigate these situations without derailing your financial goals.

1.2 Determining the ideal amount for your emergency fund: - Financial experts recommend having three to six months' worth of living expenses saved in your emergency fund. However, the appropriate amount may vary based on your personal circumstances, such as job stability, dependents, and medical needs. - Consider factors such as the stability of your income, medical history, whether you have dependents, and any ongoing financial obligations when determining the size of your emergency fund. These considerations will help you tailor your fund to suit your specific needs.

1.3 Strategies for saving and building your emergency fund: - Start by setting a specific savings goal and automate monthly contributions to your emergency fund. Treat it as a non-negotiable expense, like your rent or mortgage payment. - Cut unnecessary expenses from your budget and redirect those savings toward your emergency fund. Evaluate your current spending habits and identify areas where you can potentially reduce costs. - To build your emergency fund, consider increasing your income through side gigs or part-time work. Any extra income earned can be dedicated entirely to your emergency savings.

2. Insurance:

2.1 Understanding different types of insurance: - Insurance helps protect you financially against risks and unexpected events. Understanding the different types of insurance can help you make informed decisions about the coverage you need. - Health insurance: Protects you from high medical costs in case of illness, injury, or hospitalization. - Home insurance: Covers damages to your property caused by events like fire, theft, or natural disasters. - Car insurance: Provides coverage in case of accidents, theft, or damages to your vehicle. - Disability insurance: Offers income protection if you become disabled and unable to work. - Life insurance: Provides a payout to your beneficiaries in the event of your death.

2.2 Assessing your insurance needs and coverage: - Evaluate your current situation and identify potential risks that could have a significant financial impact. Review your insurance policies and ensure they adequately cover your needs. - Health insurance: Consider your medical history, any pre-existing conditions, and whether you have dependents that require coverage. - Home insurance: Assess the value of your home and its contents, keeping in mind potential risks specific to your area (e.g., floods, earthquakes, hurricanes). - Car insurance: Evaluate your vehicle's value and risk tolerance for potential damages or accidents. - Disability insurance: Review your income and expenses to determine the level of coverage needed to maintain financial stability in case of disability. - Life insurance: Consider your dependents' financial needs if something happens to you.

2.3 Choosing the right insurance policies for your circumstances: - Seek advice from insurance professionals or brokers who can assess your needs and recommend suitable policies. They can help you navigate the different coverage options and find the best policies for your situation. - Compare quotes and coverage from multiple insurers to ensure you get the best coverage at competitive prices. Read the policy terms and conditions carefully to understand the limitations and exclusions. - Regularly review your insurance coverage as your circumstances change. Life events such as getting married, having children, buying a house, or starting a business may necessitate adjustments to your insurance policies.

3. Creating an Emergency Plan:

3.1 Identifying potential emergencies and their financial implications: - Make a list of possible emergencies, considering both personal and external factors. This can include job loss, medical emergencies, natural disasters, major home or car repairs, or civil unrest. - Understand the financial implications of each scenario to plan better and allocate your resources. Research the costs associated with potential emergencies to estimate their financial impact on your life.

3.2 Developing a step-by-step emergency plan for various scenarios: - Create a detailed plan outlining the necessary steps to take during an emergency, considering the specific emergencies you have identified. This plan should include procedures for evacuations, contacting emergency services, and notifying loved ones. - Assign roles and responsibilities among family members or dependents, ensuring everyone knows what to do in each scenario. Practice your plan through emergency drills to familiarize everyone with their roles and ensure a smooth execution when an emergency occurs.

3.3 Communicating your emergency plan with family members or dependents: - Share your emergency plan with family members, dependents, or trusted friends. Ensure everyone understands their roles and responsibilities and knows where to find important information, such as emergency contacts, insurance policies, and relevant documents. - Review and update the plan periodically, mainly when changes in family dynamics, living situations, or potential risks occur. Regular communication and practice will ensure everyone remains prepared and aware of the plan.

4. Documenting Important Information:

4.1 Keeping copies of essential documents: - Photocopy or scan important documents such as identification, birth certificates, passports, insurance policies, property deeds, and financial records. Store physical copies and digital backups in a safe location, such as a fireproof box or encrypted digital storage. - It is also advisable to have digital copies accessible from various devices if physical copies are destroyed or inaccessible.

4.2 Storing important information in a secure and easily accessible manner: - Organize your documents and information to allow quick access during an emergency. Consider using password-protected digital platforms, encrypted USB drives, or cloud storage services that can be accessed from various devices. - Ensure your digital storage is secure by utilizing strong, unique passwords and enabling two-factor authentication. Regularly update your passwords, software, and devices with the latest security patches.

4.3 Establishing a system to access critical details during emergencies quickly: - Have a plan to retrieve and access necessary information quickly. This includes online banking login details, insurance policy numbers, contact information for doctors or emergency services, and other essential data. - Safeguard this information with secure passwords and encryption, and share access details with trusted individuals who may need to assist you during emergencies. Regularly review and update this information as needed.

5. Establishing Support Networks:

5.1 Reaching out to friends, family, or community resources for support: - Building a network of trustworthy individuals who can assist with emergencies is invaluable. Contact close friends and relatives, and consider participating in community emergency response groups or neighborhood associations. - Identify local resources such as food banks, shelters, or community organizations that can aid in times of need. Familiar5.2 Establishing a communication plan with your support network: - Create a communication plan with your support network to ensure everyone is informed and can coordinate efforts effectively during an emergency. - Exchange contact information, including phone numbers, email addresses, and social media accounts. Discuss preferred methods of communication and establish a primary and backup communication method in case of network disruptions. - Set up regular check-ins or emergency drills with your support network to maintain open lines of communication and ensure everyone is prepared.

5.3 Utilizing technology and emergency apps: - Take advantage of technology and download emergency apps that provide up-to-date information and alerts. These apps can provide real-time access to weather updates, emergency notifications, and disaster response resources. - Familiarize yourself with the app's features and understand how to use them effectively in emergencies. Please share this information with your support network so that they can also benefit from these tools.

6.   Reassessing Your Financial Plan:

6.1 Adapting your budget: - In an emergency, you may need to reassess and adjust your spending priorities. Consider reallocating funds from discretionary expenses to cover immediate needs and unexpected expenses. -

Reducing non-essential expenses and focusing on essentials such as food, shelter, utilities, and medical needs can help you stay financially stable during difficult times.

6.2 Evaluating your investment strategy: - During a financial emergency, it may be necessary to reevaluate your investment strategy and make adjustments to protect your financial stability. Consider consulting with a financial advisor to understand the best course of action for your specific situation. - Depending on the severity of the emergency, you may need to temporarily pause or adjust your investment contributions to allocate more funds towards immediate needs.

6.3 Seeking professional financial advice: - If you are in a financial crisis during an emergency, it can be beneficial to seek professional financial advice. Financial advisors can guide you in managing your finances, prioritizing expenses, and exploring potential sources of financial assistance.

Emergency planning is essential to your financial well-being, ensuring you are prepared to handle unexpected events without significant disruptions to your life and finances. Building an emergency fund, obtaining appropriate insurance coverage, creating a comprehensive emergency plan, documenting important information, establishing support networks, and reassessing your financial plan are all key steps in preparing for emergencies. By taking proactive measures and being well-prepared, you can confidently navigate emergencies and protect your financial stability.

Smart Money Habits

In this final chapter, we will delve deeper into the smart money habits that can lead to financial success and security. When followed consistently, these habits can help you build a strong financial foundation and achieve your long-term goals. So, let's explore each habit in detail:

1. Live Below Your Means: Living below your means is about spending less than you earn. It's a fundamental principle that allows you to have extra money for savings and investments. To achieve this, it's essential to create a budget that reflects your income and expenses accurately. You can start by tracking your spending for a few months to identify areas where you can cut back on non-essential items. Focus on reducing discretionary expenses such as dining out, entertainment, and impulse purchases. By making conscious choices to curb unnecessary spending, you will have the financial

freedom to save and invest for your future.

2. Set Financial Goals: Clear financial goals are the cornerstone of effective financial management. Without a direction, it's easy to fall into the trap of aimless spending and financial strain. Please write down your short-term and long-term goals, ensuring they are specific, measurable, achievable, relevant, and time-bound (SMART goals). Whether paying off debt, saving for a dream vacation, or building a retirement fund, having well-defined goals will provide focus and motivation. Break down your goals into smaller milestones to make them more manageable, and celebrate your achievements.

3. Track Your Spending: Tracking your spending is crucial to understanding where your money is going and identifying areas where you can make adjustments. Utilize budgeting tools or apps to categorize your expenses and visualize your spending patterns. This

practice lets you spot places where you may be overspending or wasting money. Divide your expenses into fixed, variable, and occasional categories to view your spending habits comprehensively. You can make informed decisions and allocate your resources more wisely by diligently tracking your expenses.

4. Automate Savings and Payments: Automating your savings and bill payments is effective for staying on track with your financial goals. Set up automatic transfers from your checking account to a dedicated savings account. Automating this process ensures that saving becomes a priority and happens without conscious effort. Additionally, consider automating your bill payments to avoid late fees or missed payments. Many banks and service providers offer automatic payment options, making staying organized and financially responsible easier. This not only saves time but also helps maintain a good credit score.

5. Prioritize Debt Repayment: If you have debt, particularly high-interest debts like credit card balances or student loans, it's crucial to prioritize their repayment. High-interest debt can hinder your financial progress and increase the overall cost of borrowing. Allocate a portion of your income towards monthly debt repayment, focusing on paying off high-interest debts first while making minimum payments on other debts. Consider implementing the debt snowball or avalanche method to gain momentum in your repayment journey. The satisfaction of seeing your debt diminish will motivate you to persevere and eventually become debt-free.

6. Build an Emergency Fund: Life is unpredictable, and financial emergencies can arise anytime. Aim to build an emergency fund with at least three to six months' living expenses to safeguard yourself and your loved ones. Please set up a separate savings account for this purpose and contribute

regularly. Start by setting an achievable target, such as saving one month's expenses, and gradually increase it until you reach your desired goal. Building an emergency fund provides a safety net, protecting you from the stress of relying on credit or loans in times of crisis.

7. Invest for the Future: Investing is key to financial growth and building wealth over time. Start investing as early as possible to take advantage of compounding interest, which allows your money to grow exponentially. Consider opening a retirement account, such as a 401(k) or an individual retirement account (IRA), and contribute consistently. Many employers offer matching contributions to retirement accounts, essentially free money. Take advantage of this opportunity to boost your retirement savings further. Additionally, explore other investment options that align with your risk tolerance and long-term goals. Educate yourself about investment

vehicles such as stocks, bonds, mutual funds, and real estate investment trusts (REITs). Seek guidance from financial advisors if needed to ensure you make informed investment decisions.

8. Be Mindful of Impulsive Buying: Impulse buying can sabotage your financial goals. Before purchasing, especially for non-essential items, take a step back and evaluate their necessity and compatibility with your financial goals. Many impulse purchases are driven by emotional triggers or the desire for instant gratification. Instead, practice delayed gratification by giving yourself time to think before making impulsive decisions. Implementing a 24-hour rule can help you overcome impulsive buying tendencies. By waiting 24 hours before purchasing, you give yourself time to assess whether it aligns with your overall financial plan. Developing mindful spending habits allows you to gain control over your finances and avoid accumulating unnecessary debt.

9. Stay Educated: Personal finance is ever-evolving, and staying informed is essential. Invest time and effort in expanding your financial knowledge through various resources. Attend workshops and seminars, read books and articles, follow reputable financial blogs, and listen to podcasts. Look for content that provides insights into budgeting, investing, debt management, tax strategies, and other relevant topics. Seek guidance from professionals, such as financial advisors and accountants, who can provide tailored advice based on your financial situation. The more knowledge you acquire, the better equipped you will be to make informed financial decisions and navigate the complexities of personal finance.

10. Surround Yourself with Like-minded Individuals: Surrounding yourself with individuals who share similar financial goals and habits can provide a supportive environment for growth. Engage in conversations about personal

finance, exchange tips, and ideas, and learn from each other's experiences. Consider joining a financial community or seeking accountability partners to hold you accountable for your financial commitments. Sharing your journey with like-minded individuals can provide motivation, support, and valuable insights. Networking with professionals in the finance industry can also provide access to expert advice and opportunities for mentorship.

Incorporating these smart money habits

It's into your daily life and requires discipline and commitment. Remember that financial health is a journey, and progress may come in small steps. Be patient with yourself and celebrate each milestone along the way. With time, dedication, and these smart money habits, you will be well on your way to achieving financial success and enjoying a more secure and prosperous future.

https://www.stylin-
spirit.com/blogs/moneymanagement/master-
brainstorming-list-for-budget-planning

Budget Planning is essential for good money
management!

Disclosure - I am not a financial or tax expert.
When implementing any solid financial
strategy, it is good to get help from experts.

Master Brainstorming List for Budget Planning

The process of budgeting, one of the crucial
types of budgets, begins with assessing needs
versus wants, which is a critical step in
creating a good budget plan. To understand
how to budget money, start by making a
comprehensive list of assumptions about your
monthly budget, detailing each item as much
as possible. This budget breakdown will allow
you to evaluate each expenditure on its
merits, providing you with a clear view of how
to effectively allocate your money. By
thoroughly understanding the alternative
decisions you can make, you will be able to

avoid potential problems in managing personal finances. This budgeting method, often seen in budget examples like the zero-based budget, is widely recognized as a key financial tip for maintaining a healthy home budget. It emphasizes the importance of being intentional and deliberate with your spending choices, a crucial aspect of money management tips.

Housing Costs

Mortgages or rent/lease payments:

Principal

Interest

Homeowners Insurance/renters insurance

Understanding the Components of Housing Costs

When considering whether refinancing is a viable option, it is crucial to have a comprehensive understanding of the various components that make up housing costs. One of the most significant factors to take into account is the mortgage rates, which represents the cost of borrowing money. This interest is the amount charged by the bank or lending company for allowing you to use their funds, and it is repaid over a specific period, typically ranging from 15 to 30 years. It might surprise you to learn that the larger the personal loans and the longer the repayment period, the more you end up paying in interest compared to the actual value of the asset.

When applying for a home loan, it is essential to ensure that there are no prepayment penalties. This is because prepayment penalties can restrict your ability to make principal-only payments, which can significantly reduce the overall interest paid on the loan and shorten its duration. A good strategy to consider is aiming to make an extra payment per year on your mortgage, as this can help you save a substantial amount of money in the long run, a key aspect of effective debt repayment.

A commonly used rule of thumb is that refinancing may be worthwhile if you can lower the mortgage rates on your home loan by at least 1%. However, it is important to note that if you are currently facing cash flow issues, extending the personal loan period may provide temporary relief, although it will ultimately increase the overall cost of financing over the lifetime of the loan.

Another important aspect to consider when it comes to housing costs is home insurance. The cost of homeowners insurance is influenced by several factors, including deductibles, liability coverage, supplemental coverage for valuable items such as art or jewelry, and the expenses associated with rebuilding in the event of loss or damage. It is crucial to review and update these considerations annually to account for inflation and ensure that you are adequately protected and not underinsured.

For those who rent or lease their residence, it is equally important to carefully review the rental or lease agreement to ensure that your home insurance coverage adequately protects you from potential losses. It is worth noting that the homeowner's insurance policy of the property owner typically does not cover your personal possessions unless explicitly stated in your agreement.

By understanding the various components of housing costs, such as mortgage rates, prepayment penalties, and home insurance coverage, you can make informed decisions about refinancing and ensure that you are adequately protected financially. Taking the time to review and update these factors regularly, including the terms of your personal loans, will help you stay on top of your housing costs and make the most financially sound choices for your situation.

Home equity loans or line of credit payments

Homeowners Association Dues

Sewer

Water

Landscaping maintenance

The cost of landscaping can fluctuate significantly throughout the year, depending on the climate of the area you live in. This is an important consideration when planning your landscaping project. Factors such as seasonal changes, weather conditions, and the specific needs of the plants and materials you choose can influence the expenses associated with maintaining and beautifying your outdoor space. For instance, in regions with harsh winters, you may need to invest in winterizing your garden or protecting delicate plants from frost damage. Conversely, in areas with hot and dry summers, considerations like irrigation systems or drought-resistant plants might be necessary to ensure the longevity and vitality of your landscape. By comprehending the impact of climate on landscaping costs, you can make informed decisions and create a beautiful outdoor space that thrives in your specific environment.

Pet control

Natural Gas

Propane (for rural homes)

Electricity

Cable, satellite, dish, streaming or other subscription costs

Internet

Phone (Landline and or cell phone)

Utility providers often raise their rates periodically, influenced by both long-term trends and seasonal fluctuations. If managing your monthly expenses is a concern, opting for level payments throughout the year could prove beneficial. Many utility companies offer this option, but you can also independently implement this strategy to manage your fixed expenses. For example, in regions with warmer climates, the cost of air conditioning tends to rise sharply during the summer months. By spreading out your payments evenly over the year, you can better anticipate and manage these increased expenses, ensuring a more stable financial situation.

Home Maintenance

A home repair fund (for the breakdown of equipment)

Understanding the age of your appliances, air conditioning, and furnace can provide valuable information for your savings accounts and investment accounts. This knowledge allows you to anticipate when they might require maintenance or replacement, helping you plan and budget accordingly. Furthermore, it can help you make informed decisions about energy efficiency. Older appliances and HVAC systems are often less energy-efficient than newer models, leading to higher utility bills. By knowing the age of these items, you can assess whether investing in newer, more energy-efficient alternatives is more cost-effective. This knowledge empowers you to maintain the functionality and efficiency of your household appliances, air conditioning, and furnace, saving you time, money, and potential headaches in the long run.

Home maintenance (annual furnace tune-up, lawn care, gardening, etc.)

A home upgrade/remodel fund (new appliances, painting needs, etc.)

A new furniture fund

Tax preparation and legal fees

Vehicle and Transportation Costs

Vehicle purchase payments or lease payments

Auto insurance premiums

Insurance deductibles

Fuel costs

Public transportation

Parking expenses

A vehicle maintenance fund (oil changes, car washes, new tires, wiper fluid, etc.)

Toll fees

Vehicle registration and DMV costs

A vehicle repair fund (to fund future vehicle repair costs)

Vehicle storage costs

Transportation costs specific to your commute

Parking fees

Groceries & Household supplies

General groceries and cleaning supplies

Social/family gatherings

Holiday food funds

Eating out (including lunch for work)

First-aid supplies

Vitamins and other health supplements

Non-prescription (over the counter) medicines

Haircare products

Employment Related Expenses

Work clothing/uniforms

Dry cleaning expenses

Client gifts and other client expenses

Professional fees

Licensing costs (if applicable)

Continuing education costs

Work travel expenses

Coworker gifts and celebration related expenses

Work-related social gatherings

Health and Medical

A clinic and hospital copay fund

Prescription medicines

Dental care costs

Eye care costs

Naturopathic, homeopathic and alternative health costs

Medical equipment

Orthodontic care

Out-of-pocket deductibles

Health insurance premiums

HSA and FSA contributions

New baby/child medical expenses

Annual Checkups and Copays

Personal Care

Clothing purchases

Haircuts and other salon services

Beauty products such as makeup and fragrances

Athletic gear like running shoes

Health club membership fees

Fun money (for friend and other miscellaneous gatherings)

Self-care activity money (anything you do to rejuvenate and refresh)

Hobby expenses

Children and Dependents

Childcare expenses (daycare and babysitters/nannies)

Clothing

Haircuts and other grooming costs

School supplies

School lunches

Sports and extracurricular activities

Summer camps

Toys and learning activities

Miscellaneous social/friend outings

Baby formula, diapers and other baby costs

Allowances

Pet Care

Pet purchase fund

Pet food

Annual vet costs (check-ups, vaccinations, dewormer, etc.)

Emergency vet costs

Pet insurance (if applicable)

Training costs (if applicable)

Pet boarding/pet care costs

Grooming costs

City/county pet license costs

Other pet supplies (toys, leashes, litter supplies, etc.)

Holiday, Family and Religion

Tithing to your local church other religious organization

Charitable donations to causes you support

Birthday gifts

Anniversary gifts

Wedding gifts

Graduation gifts

Holiday gifts such as Easter, Christmas or Hanukkah

Bar Mitzvah, baptism or other religious celebration gifts

Giving to your community

Social and Entertainment

Theatre, opera and other shows

Music concerts

Day trips

Museum and historical society membership dues

Camping, hiking and other nature excursions

Holiday events

Family gatherings and events

Summer gatherings such as BBQs

Friend gatherings

Sporting events (viewing)

Participatory sporting events (marathons, fun runs)

Weekend getaways

Summer vacations

Winter vacations

Debt Service other than Mortgage

Student loan payments

Credit card payments

Being aware of your credit score and monitoring credit card promotions is beneficial as it keeps you informed about the various options available. By staying updated with the market, you may find opportunities to transfer your outstanding balance to a different lender offering a more reasonable interest rate. Some lenders may even offer promotional introductory periods with zero percent interest options, which can be highly beneficial for credit consolidation. If you find yourself in significant credit card debt, considering home equity loans to reduce your interest expenses might be worthwhile. However, maintaining healthy spending habits is crucial to protect yourself against overwhelming debt. While unavoidable emergencies can occur, being financially responsible can help mitigate their impact.

Auto loan payments

Other personal loan payments

Repayment of loans from family

Loans for recreational vehicles

Insurance

Term Life Insurance

Auto Insurance

Health Insurance

Income Protection Insurance

Long-Term Disability Insurance

Long-Term Care Insurance (if you're age 60 or older)

Identity Theft Insurance

Business Insurance

Umbrella Policy (if you have a net worth of $500,000 or more)

Investing and Retirement

Emergency fund savings

401k savings

IRA or other retirement savings

Non-retirement investment funds

Transaction fees

Brokerage fees

Other

Upgraded house fund

Replacement car fund

Vacation fund

College savings (for yourself, your children or your grandchildren)

Financial independence/retire early fund

Other sinking fund purposes

Conclusion

Managing your financial obligations is crucial for maintaining a stable and secure future. It is important to prioritize your expenses and be mindful of your spending habits in order to effectively allocate your resources towards debt service, insurance, investing, and other important financial goals. By carefully managing your finances, you can ensure that you are making the most of your income and minimizing unnecessary expenses.

One way to achieve this is by regularly monitoring your credit score. Your credit score is a reflection of your creditworthiness and can impact your ability to secure loans or obtain favorable interest rates. By keeping an eye on your credit score, you can identify any areas for improvement and take steps to build a strong credit history.

Another strategy to consider is exploring options for credit consolidation. Consolidating your debts can help you streamline your payments and potentially reduce the overall interest expenses. This can make it easier to manage your debt and ultimately pay it off more quickly.

In addition to managing debt, it is also important to have appropriate insurance coverage. Insurance provides financial protection in the event of unexpected events such as accidents, illnesses, or natural disasters. By having the right insurance policies in place, you can safeguard yourself and your loved ones from potential financial hardships.

Furthermore, building a solid retirement fund is essential for long-term financial security. Planning for retirement early and consistently contributing to a retirement account can help ensure that you have enough funds to support yourself in your golden years.

By making informed and responsible financial decisions, you can achieve financial stability and peace of mind. Taking the time to assess your financial situation, prioritize your expenses, and explore options for credit consolidation and insurance coverage can go a long way in securing your financial future. Remember, it is never too early or too late to start taking control of your finances and working towards a stable and secure future.